HE PHILLIP KEVEREN SERIES   PIANO SOLO

BLUES CLASSICS

15 OF THE BEST ARRANGED BY PHILLIP KEVEREN

— PIANO LEVEL —
LATE INTERMEDIATE/EARLY ADVANCED

ISBN 978-1-4950-7669-5

HAL•LEONARD®
7777 W. BLUEMOUND RD. P.O. BOX 13819 MILWAUKEE, WI 53213

For all works contained herein:
Unauthorized copying, arranging, adapting, recording, Internet posting, public performance,
or other distribution of the printed music in this publication is an infringement of copyright.
Infringers are liable under the law.

Visit Hal Leonard Online at
www.halleonard.com

Visit Phillip at
www.phillipkeveren.com

PREFACE

Originated by African Americans in the Deep South, the blues incorporates spirituals, shouts, and chants into a genre that is wholly unique in its musical character. Blue notes (usually the lowered third, fifth, and seventh steps of the major scale) are integral to its melancholy melodies. Standard eight- and twelve-bar chord progressions are often part of the harmonic structure of the blues.

This collection covers a wide variety of blues expressions, and I am indebted to Jeff Schroedl at Hal Leonard for his expert guidance in the assembly of its contents.

Phillip Keveren

BIOGRAPHY

Phillip Keveren, a multi-talented keyboard artist and composer, has composed original works in a variety of genres from piano solo to symphonic orchestra. Mr. Keveren gives frequent concerts and workshops for teachers and their students in the United States, Canada, Europe, and Asia. Mr. Keveren holds a B.M. in composition from California State University Northridge and a M.M. in composition from the University of Southern California.

CONTENTS

BASIN STREET BLUES

Words and Music by
SPENCER WILLIAMS
Arranged by Phillip Keveren

© 1928, 1929, 1933 (Renewed) EDWIN H. MORRIS & COMPANY, A Division of MPL Music Publishing, Inc.
This arrangement © 2017 EDWIN H. MORRIS & COMPANY, A Division of MPL Music Publishing, Inc.
All Rights Reserved

6

CALDONIA
(What Makes Your Big Head So Hard?)

Words and Music by
FLEECIE MOORE
Arranged by Phillip Keveren

© 1945 (Renewed) CHERIO CORP.
This arrangement © 2017 CHERIO CORP.
All Rights Reserved

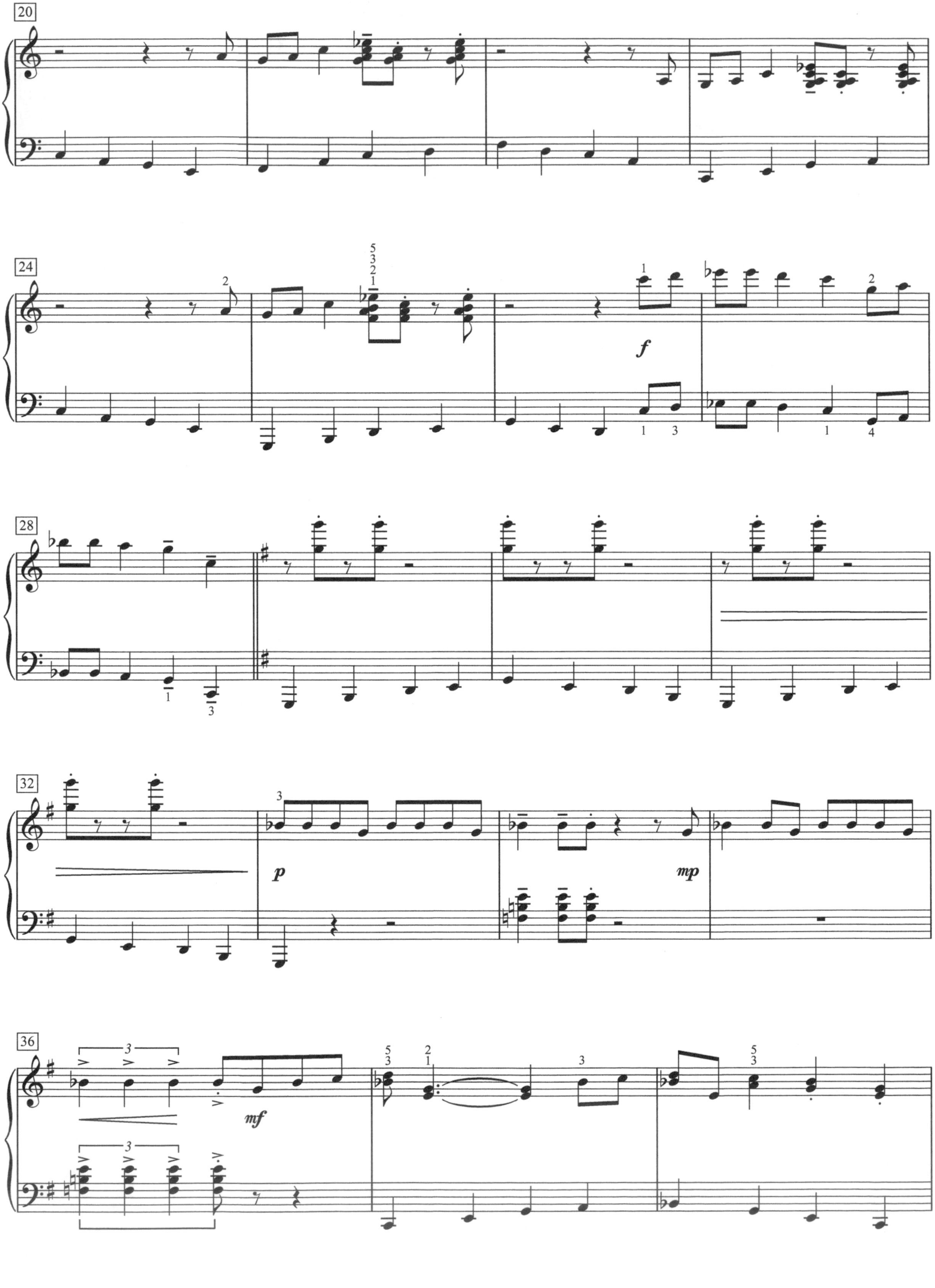
20
24
f
28
32
p
mp
36
mf

DARLIN' YOU KNOW I LOVE YOU

Words and Music by B.B. KING
and JULES BIHARI
Arranged by Phillip Keveren

Copyright © 1953 by Universal Music - Careers
Copyright Renewed
This arrangement Copyright © 2017 by Universal Music - Careers
International Copyright Secured   All Rights Reserved

EVERY DAY I HAVE THE BLUES

Words and Music by
PETER CHATMAN
Arranged by Phillip Keveren

Copyright © 1952; Renewed 1980 Arc Music Corp., Trio Music Company and Fort Knox Music Inc.
This arrangement Copyright © 2017 Arc Music Corp., Trio Music Company and Fort Knox Music Inc.
All Rights for Arc Music Corp. and Trio Music Company Administered by BMG Rights Management (US) LLC
International Copyright Secured   All Rights Reserved

FEVER

Words and Music by JOHN DAVENPORT
and EDDIE COOLEY
Arranged by Phillip Keveren

Copyright © 1956 Trio Music Company and Fort Knox Music Inc.
Copyright Renewed
This arrangement Copyright © 2017 Trio Music Company and Fort Knox Music Inc.
All Rights for Trio Music Company Administered by BMG Rights Management (US) LLC
All Rights Reserved   Used by Permission

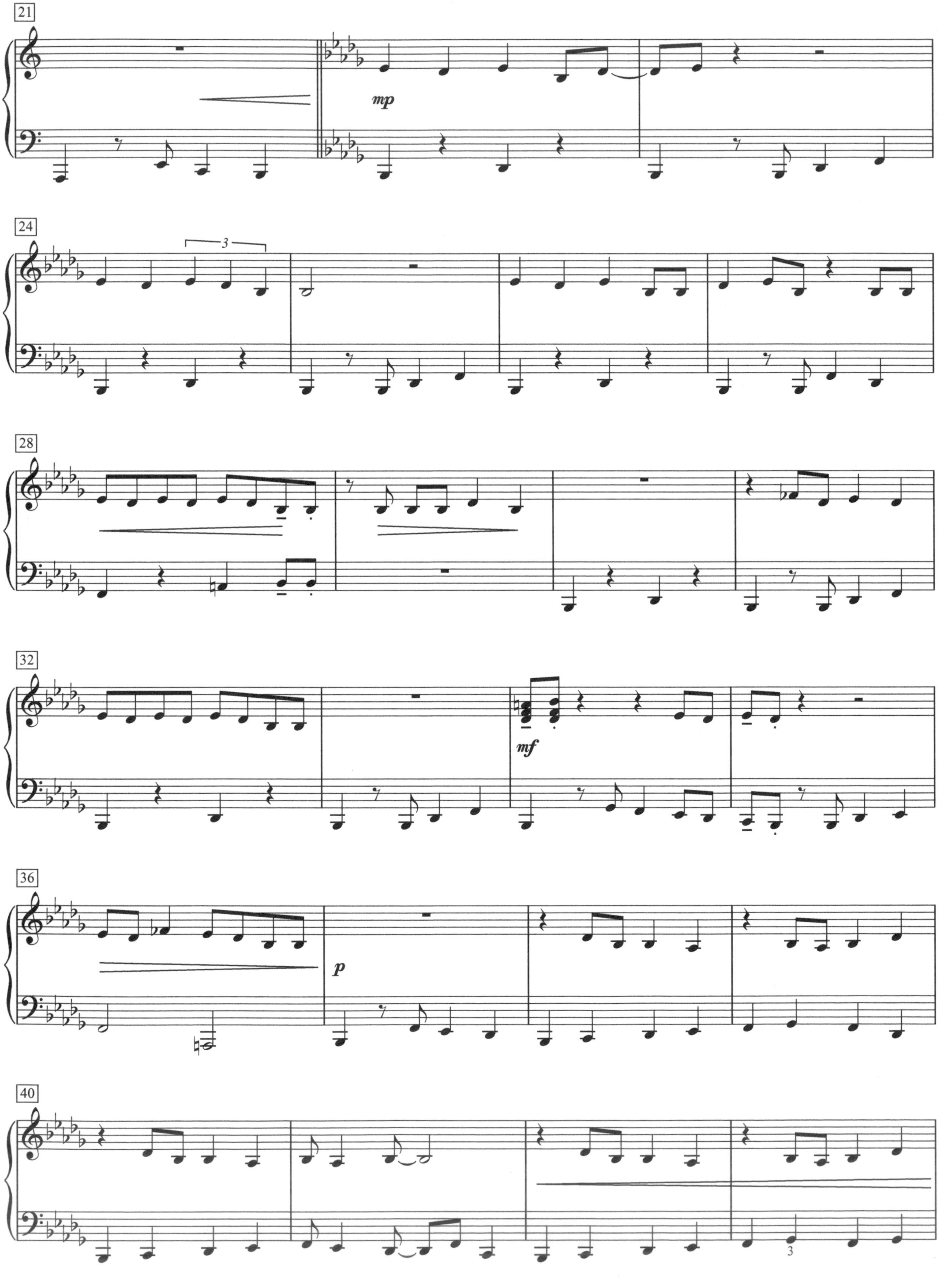
21
mp
24
3
28
32
mf
36
p
40

I GOT IT BAD AND THAT AIN'T GOOD

Words by PAUL FRANCIS WEBSTER
Music by DUKE ELLINGTON
Arranged by Phillip Keveren

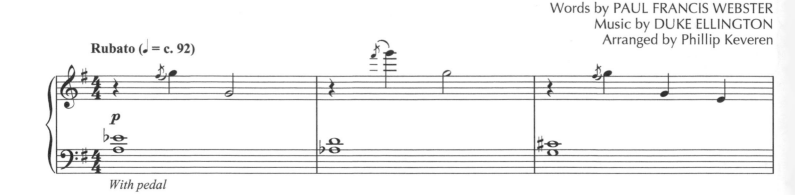

Copyright © 1941 Sony/ATV Music Publishing LLC and Webster Music Co. in the U.S.A.
Copyright Renewed
This arrangement Copyright © 2017 Sony/ATV Music Publishing LLC and Webster Music Co. in the U.S.A.
All Rights on behalf of Sony/ATV Music Publishing LLC Administered by Sony/ATV Music Publishing LLC, 424 Church Street, Suite 1200, Nashville, TN 37219
Rights for the world outside the U.S.A. Administered by EMI Robbins Catalog Inc. (Publishing) and Alfred Music (Print)
International Copyright Secured   All Rights Reserved

IT HURTS ME TOO

Words and Music by
MEL LONDON
Arranged by Phillip Keveren

Slow Blues (♩. = 60)

Copyright © 1957 Conrad Music and Lonmel Publishing
Copyright Renewed
This arrangement Copyright © 2017 Conrad Music and Lonmel Publishing
All Rights Administered by BMG Rights Management (US) LLC
All Rights Reserved   Used by Permission

21

KANSAS CITY

Words and Music by JERRY LEIBER
and MIKE STOLLER
Arranged by Phillip Keveren

Copyright © 1952 Sony/ATV Music Publishing LLC
Copyright Renewed
This arrangement Copyright © 2017 Sony/ATV Music Publishing LLC
All Rights Administered by Sony/ATV Music Publishing LLC, 424 Church Street, Suite 1200, Nashville, TN 37219
International Copyright Secured   All Rights Reserved

NIGHT TRAIN

Words by OSCAR WASHINGTON and
LEWIS C. SIMPKINS
Music by JIMMY FORREST
Arranged by Phillip Keveren

Copyright © 1952 (Renewed) by Embassy Music Corporation (BMI)
This arrangement Copyright © 2017 by Embassy Music Corporation (BMI)
International Copyright Secured   All Rights Reserved
Reprinted by Permission

KIDNEY STEW BLUES

Words and Music by LEONA BLACKMAN
and EDDIE VINSON
Arranged by Phillip Keveren

© 1947 (Renewed) CHERIO CORP.
This arrangement © 2016 CHERIO CORP.
All Rights Reserved

MY BABE

Written by WILLIE DIXON
Arranged by Phillip Keveren

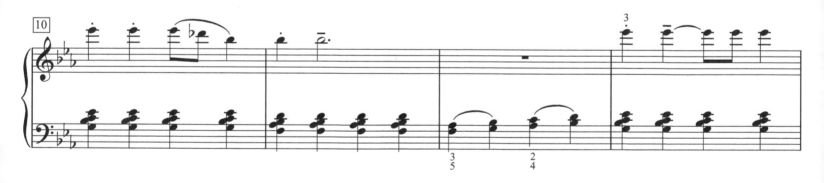

Copyright © 1955 Hoochie Coochie Music
Copyright Renewed
This arrangement Copyright © 2017 Hoochie Coochie Music
All Rights Administered by BMG Rights Management (US) LLC
All Rights Reserved   Used by Permission

NOBODY KNOWS YOU
WHEN YOU'RE DOWN AND OUT

Words and Music by
JIMMIE COX
Arranged by Phillip Keveren

Copyright © 1923, 1929, 1950, 1959, 1963 UNIVERSAL MUSIC CORP.
Copyright Renewed
This arrangement Copyright © 2017 UNIVERSAL MUSIC CORP.
All Rights Reserved   Used by Permission

STORMY WEATHER
(Keeps Rainin' All the Time)
from COTTON CLUB PARADE OF 1933

Words by TED KOEHLER
Music by HAROLD ARLEN
Arranged by Phillip Keveren

Copyright © 1933 Fred Ahlert Music Group, Ted Koehler Music Co. and S.A. Music Co.
Copyright Renewed
This arrangement Copyright © 2017 Fred Ahlert Music Group, Ted Koehler Music Co. and S.A. Music Co.
All Rights for Fred Ahlert Music Group and Ted Koehler Music Co. Administered by BMG Rights Management (US) LLC
All Rights Reserved   Used by Permission

SWEET HOME CHICAGO

Words and Music by
ROBERT JOHNSON
Arranged by Phillip Keveren

Copyright © (1978), 1990, 1991 Standing Ovation and Encore Music (SESAC)
This arrangement Copyright © 2017 Standing Ovation and Encore Music (SESAC)
Under license from The Bicycle Music Company
All Rights Reserved

ROUTE 66

By BOBBY TROUP
Arranged by Phillip Keveren

Copyright © 1946, Renewed 1973, Assigned 1974 to Londontown Music
This arrangement Copyright © 2017 Londontown Music
All Rights outside the U.S.A. controlled by Edwin H. Morris & Company, A Division of MPL Music Publishing, Inc.
International Copyright Secured   All Rights Reserved

BOOK ONE

CHRISTMAS PIANO SOLOS

JOHN THOMPSON'S
ADULT PIANO COURSE

The Christmas songs in this collection were arranged and edited with the adult student in mind. They are perfectly suited to the student learning from *John Thompson's Adult Piano Course (Book 1)*, but are also appropriate for students learning from any method, or for anyone playing the piano for personal pleasure and enjoyment.

CONTENTS

Wonderful Christmastime

With *John Thompson's Adult Piano Course (Book 1)*, use after page 11.

Words and Music by
Paul McCartney
Arranged by Eric Baumgartner

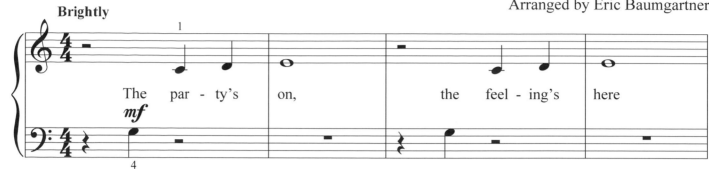

The par - ty's on, the feel - ing's here

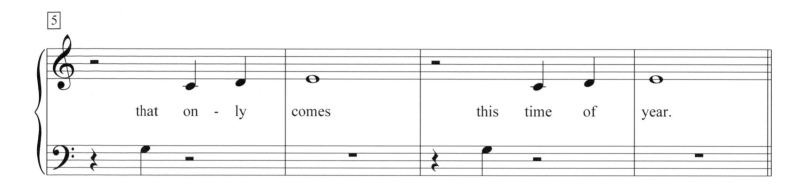

that on - ly comes this time of year.

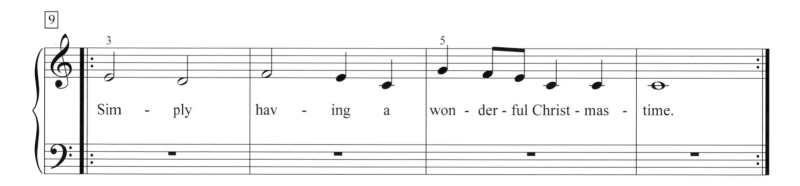

Sim - ply hav - ing a won - der - ful Christ - mas - time.

Accompaniment (Student plays one octave higher than written.)

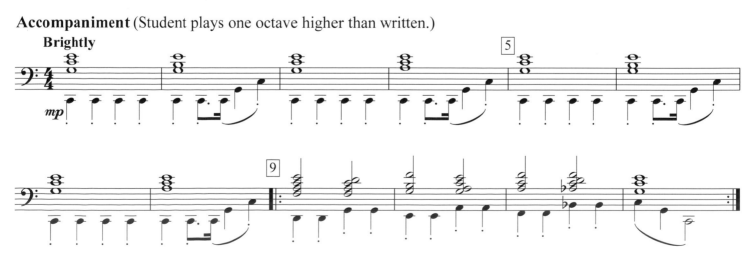

© 1979 MPL COMMUNICATIONS LTD.
This arrangement © 2009 MPL COMMUNICATIONS LTD.
Administered by MPL COMMUNICATIONS, INC.
All Rights Reserved

Do You Hear What I Hear

Use after page 13.

Words and Music by Noel Regney
and Gloria Shayne
Arranged by Eric Baumgartner

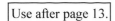

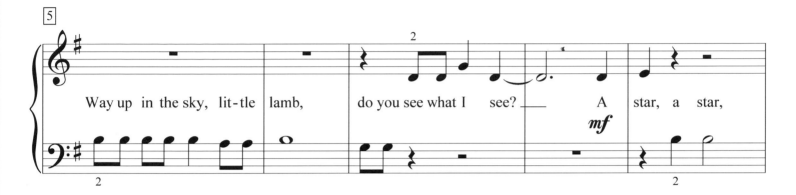

Accompaniment (Student plays one octave higher than written.)

Copyright © 1962 (Renewed) by Jewel Music Publishing Co., Inc. (ASCAP)
This arrangement Copyright © 2006 by Jewel Music Publishing Co., Inc. (ASCAP)
International Copyright Secured   All Rights Reserved
Used by Permission

Blue Christmas

Use after page 15.

Words and Music by Billy Hayes
and Jay Johnson
Arranged by Carolyn Miller

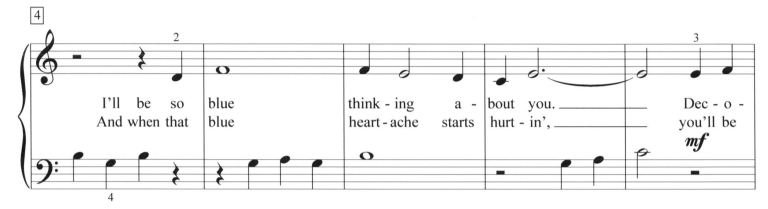

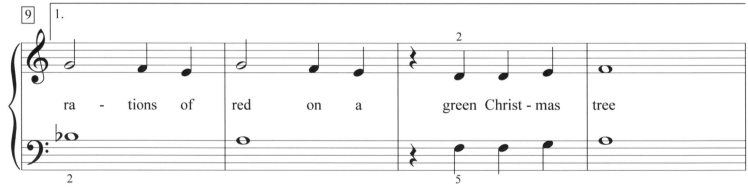

Accompaniment (Student plays one octave higher than written.)

Copyright © 1948 UNIVERSAL - POLYGRAM INTERNATIONAL PUBLISHING, INC. and JUDY J. OLMSTEAD TRUST
Copyright Renewed
This arrangement Copyright © 2008 UNIVERSAL - POLYGRAM INTERNATIONAL PUBLISHING, INC. and JUDY J. OLMSTEAD TRUST
All Rights for JUDY J. OLMSTEAD TRUST Controlled and Administered by LICHELLE MUSIC COMPANY
All Rights Reserved   Used by Permission

won't mean a thing   if   you're not here with   me. I'll have a
mp

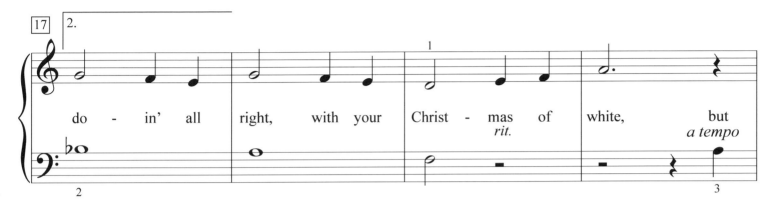

do - in' all right,   with your   Christ - mas of   white,   but
rit.   *a tempo*

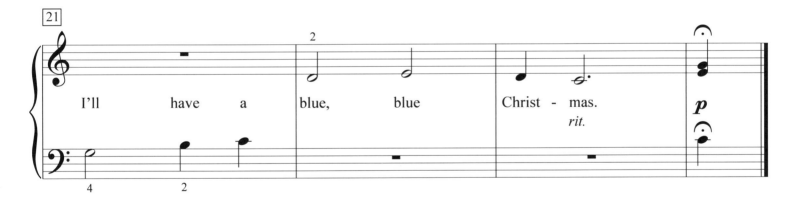

I'll   have a   blue,   blue   Christ - mas.
rit.   *p*

rit.   *a tempo*   *rit.*

I'll Be Home for Christmas

Use after page 23.

Words and Music by Kim Gannon
and Walter Kent
Arranged by Eric Baumgartner

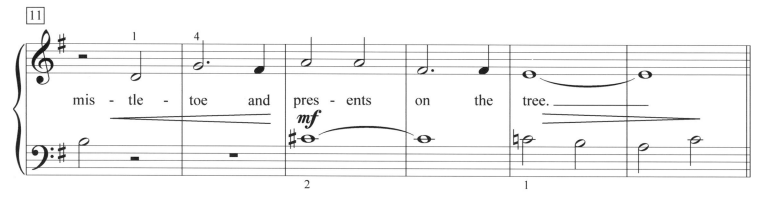

Accompaniment (Student plays one octave higher than written.)

© Copyright 1943 by GANNON & KENT MUSIC CO., Inc., Beverly Hills, CA
Copyright Renewed
This arrangement © Copyright 2006 by Gannon & Kent Music Co., Inc.
International Copyright Secured   All Rights Reserved

9

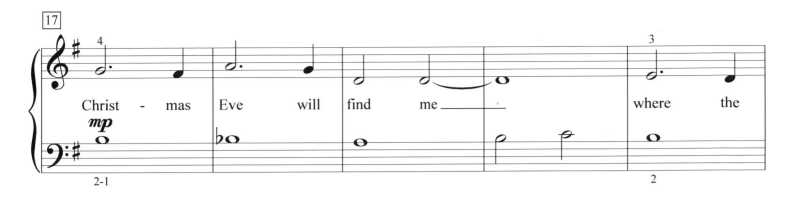

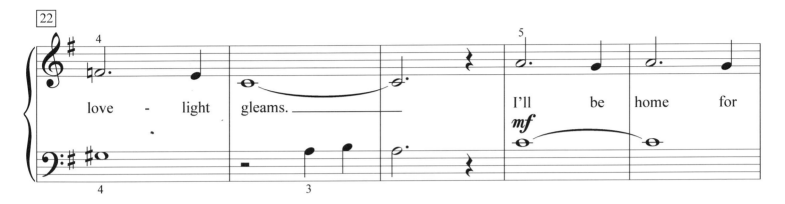

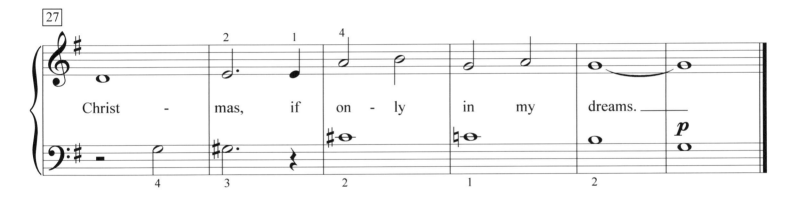

Mister Santa

Use after page 27.

Words and Music by Pat Ballard
Arranged by Carolyn Miller

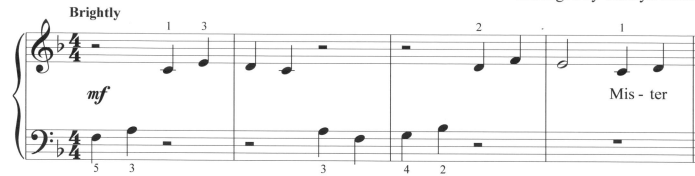

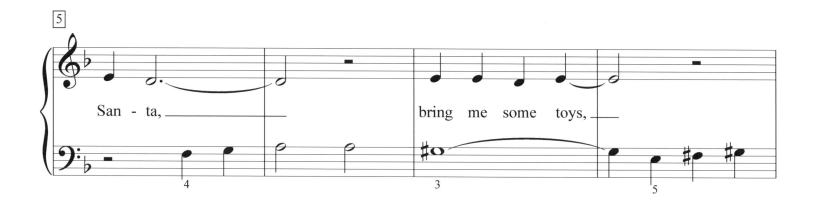

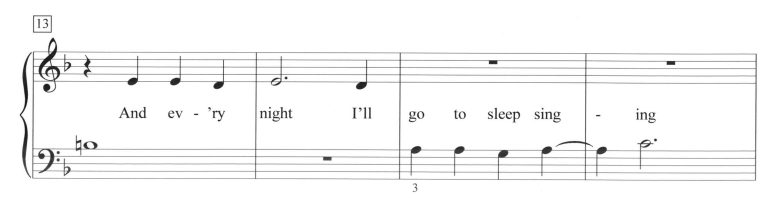

© 1954, 1955 (Renewed) EDWIN H. MORRIS & COMPANY, A Division of MPL Music Publishing, Inc.
This arrangement © 2014 EDWIN H. MORRIS & COMPANY, A Division of MPL Music Publishing, Inc.
All Rights Reserved

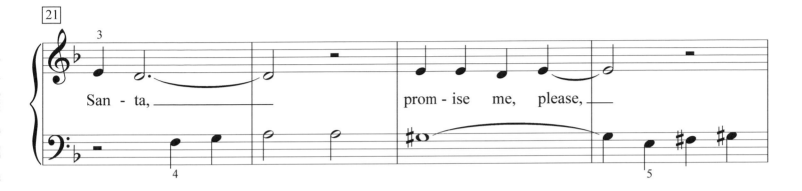

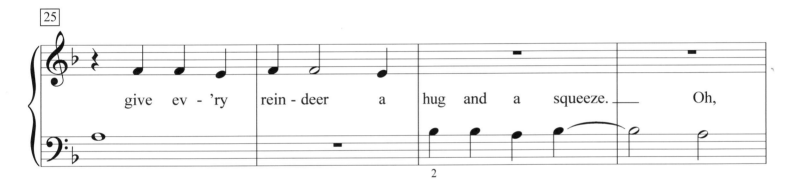

Christmas
(Baby Please Come Home)

Use after page 38.

Words and Music by Phil Spector,
Ellie Greenwich and Jeff Barry
Arranged by Glenda Austin

Copyright © 1963 Trio Music Company, Universal - Songs Of PolyGram International, Inc., Abkco Music Inc. and Mother Bertha Music, Inc.
Copyright Renewed
This arrangement Copyright © 2016 Trio Music Company, Universal - Songs Of PolyGram International, Inc., Abkco Music Inc. and Mother Bertha Music, Inc.
All Rights for Trio Music Company Controlled and Administered by BMG Rights Management (US) LLC
All Rights for Abkco Music Inc. and Mother Bertha Music, Inc. Administered by Sony/ATV Music Publishing LLC, 424 Church Street, Suite 1200, Nashville, TN 37219
All Rights Reserved   Used by Permissions

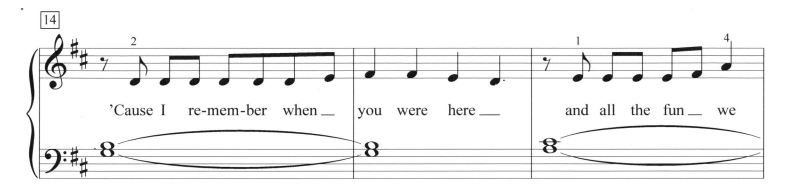

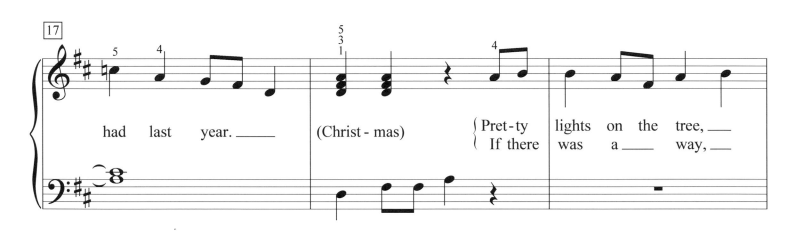

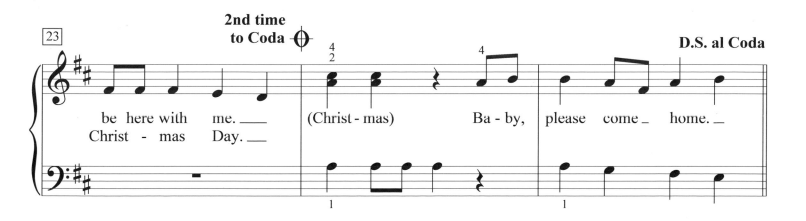

14

CODA

(Please)   Please, _   (please)   please, _

(please)   please, _   (please)   please, _   (please)   ba - by, please   come

rit.

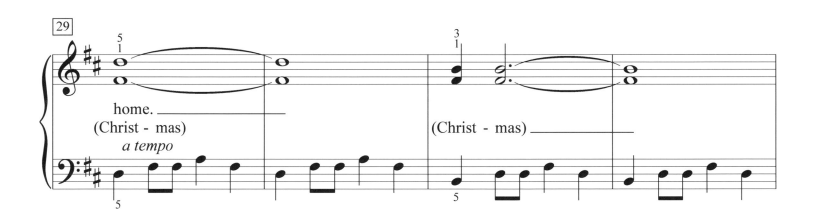

home. _____
(Christ - mas) _____   (Christ - mas) _____

a tempo

(Christ - mas) _____   (Christ - mas)

rit.

I Heard the Bells on Christmas Day

Use after page 45.

Words by Henry Wadsworth Longfellow
Adapted by Johnny Marks
Music by Johnny Marks
Arranged by Eric Baumgartner

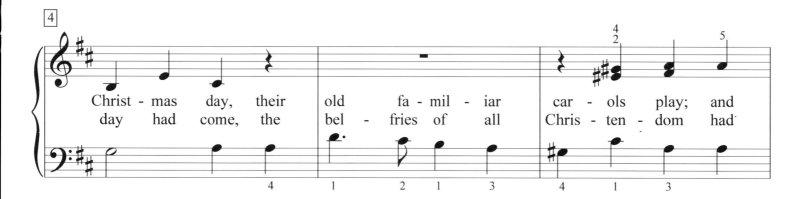

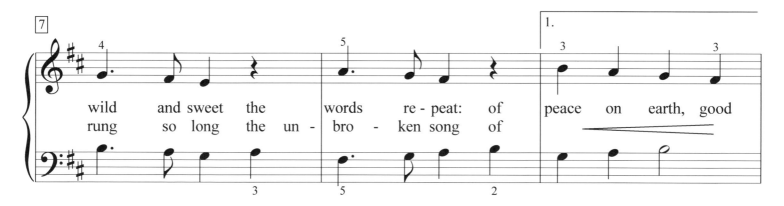

Copyright © 1956 (Renewed 1984) St. Nicholas Music Inc., 254 W. 54th Street, 12th Floor, New York, New York 10019
This arrangement Copyright © 2016 St. Nicholas Music Inc.
All Rights Reserved

O Holy Night

Use after page 55.

French Words by Placide Cappeau
English Words by John S. Dwight
Music by Adolphe Adam
Arranged by Glenda Austin

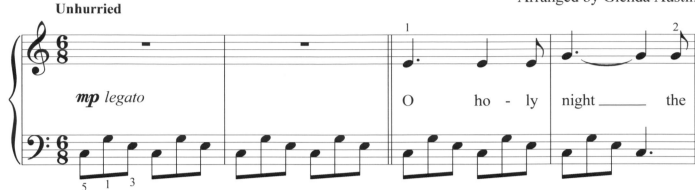

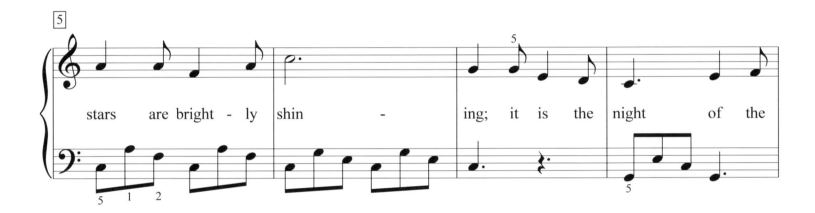

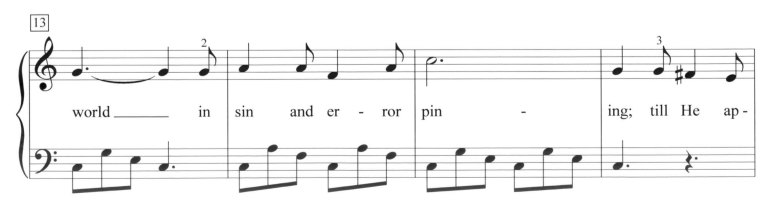

© 2016 by The Willis Music Co.
International Copyright Secured   All Rights Reserved

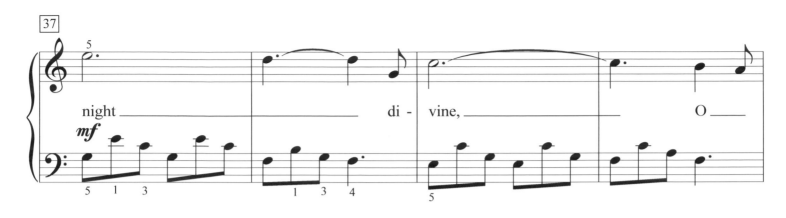

night _____ di - vine, _____ O _____

night _____ when Christ was born! O night _____

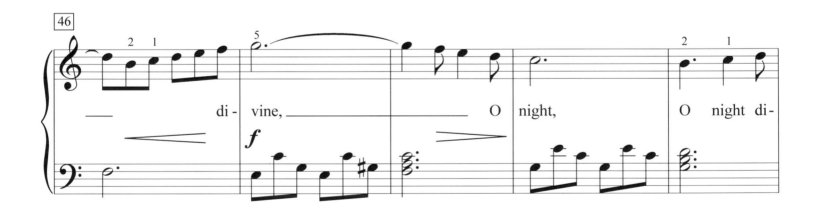

_____ di - vine, _____ O night, O night di-

vine. rit.

Feliz Navidad

Use after page 63.

Music and Lyrics by José Feliciano
Arranged by Carolyn Miller

Moderately, with a lilt

mf Fe-liz Na-vi-dad. Fe-liz Na-vi-dad.

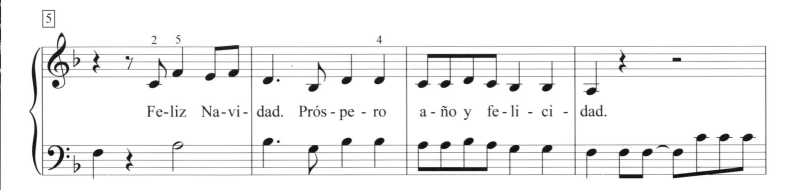

Fe-liz Na-vi-dad. Prós-pe-ro a-ño y fe-li-ci-dad.

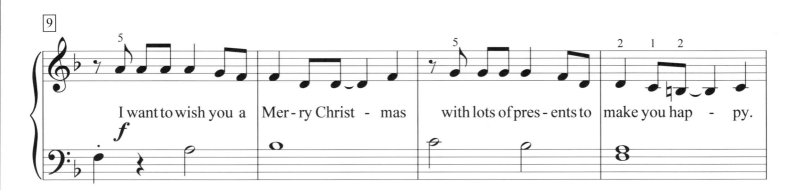

I want to wish you a Mer-ry Christ-mas with lots of pres-ents to make you hap-py.

f

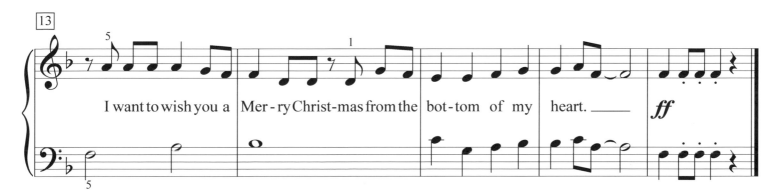

I want to wish you a Mer-ry Christ-mas from the bot-tom of my heart.

ff

Copyright © 1970 J & H Publishing Company (ASCAP)
Copyright Renewed
This arrangement Copyright © 2016 J & H Publishing Company (ASCAP)
All Rights Administered by Law, P.A. o/b/o J & H Publishing Company
International Copyright Secured   All Rights Reserved

Christmas Time Is Here
from A CHARLIE BROWN CHRISTMAS

Use after page 69.

Words by Lee Mendelson
Music by Vince Guaraldi
Arranged by Eric Baumgartner

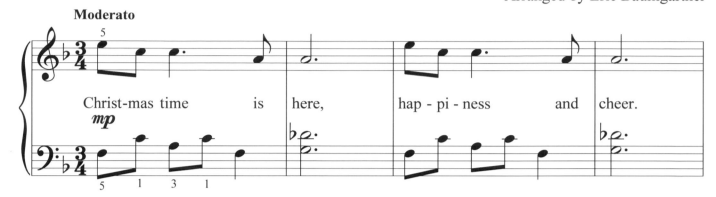

Christ-mas time is here, hap-pi-ness and cheer.

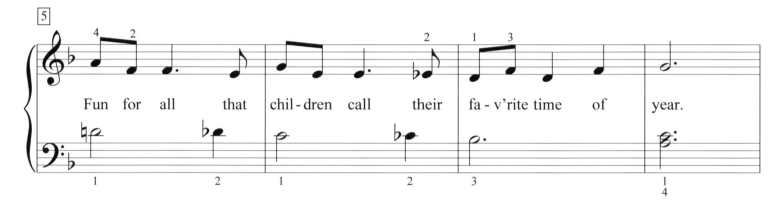

Fun for all that chil-dren call their fa-v'rite time of year.

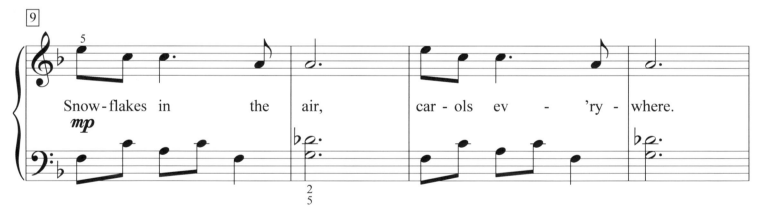

Snow-flakes in the air, car-ols ev-'ry-where.

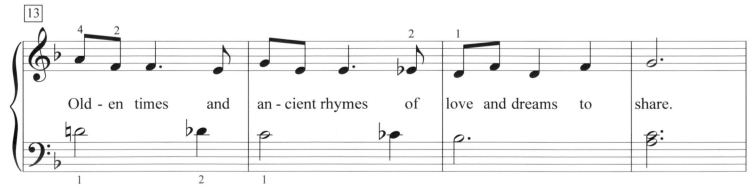

Old-en times and an-cient rhymes of love and dreams to share.

Copyright © 1966 LEE MENDELSON FILM PRODUCTIONS, INC.
Copyright Renewed
This arrangement Copyright © 2006 LEE MENDELSON FILM PRODUCTIONS, INC.
International Copyright Secured   All Rights Reserved

21

Silver Bells

from the Paramount Picture THE LEMON DROP KID

Use after page 73.

Words and Music by Jay Livingston
and Ray Evans
Arranged by Carolyn Miller

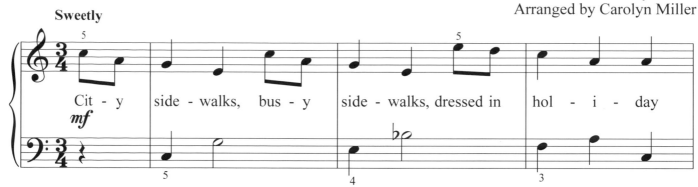

City sidewalks, busy sidewalks, dressed in holiday

style. In the air there's a feeling of Christmas.

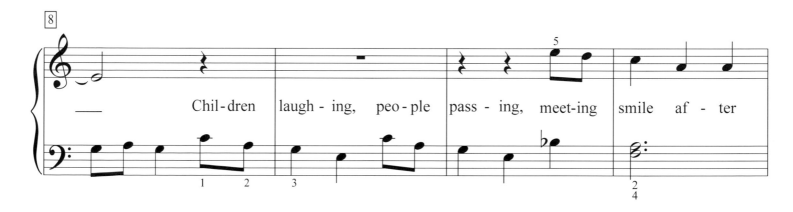

Children laughing, people passing, meeting smile after

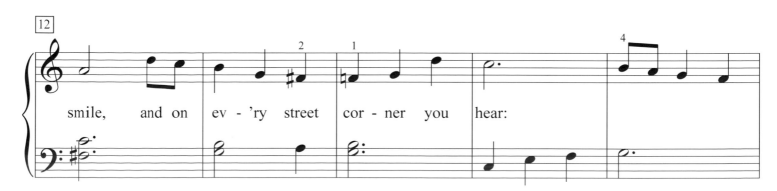

smile, and on ev'ry street corner you hear:

Copyright © 1950 Sony/ATV Music Publishing LLC
Copyright Renewed
This arrangement Copyright © 2008 Sony/ATV Music Publishing LLC
All Rights Administered by Sony/ATV Music Publishing LLC, 424 Church Street, Suite 1200, Nashville, TN 37219
International Copyright Secured   All Rights Reserved

23

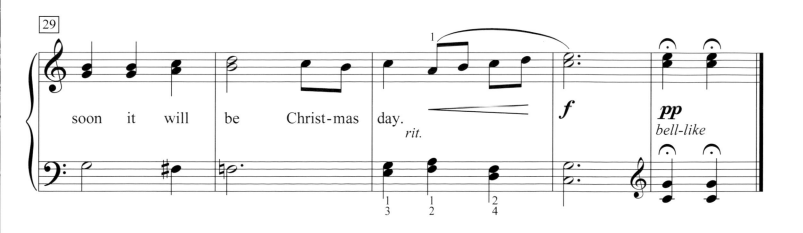

Dance of the Sugar Plum Fairy

from THE NUTCRACKER

Use after page 79.

By Pyotr Il'yich Tchaikovsky
Arranged by Glenda Austin

© 2016 by The Willis Music Co.
International Copyright Secured   All Rights Reserved